Fairies Taste Like Machine Gun

Andrew Zosangzuala

Published by Golden Leaf Haven Publishing, 2024.

Published by Golden Leaf Haven Publishing,
36 Saint John's Place
Freeport 11520-4618
New York, USA

Airhub 1425, UBX 6 Poyle Trading Estate,
Colndale Road, Colnbrook
Slough SL30AA
Berkshire, United Kingdom

Table of Contents

Memento Mori 1

Cosmos In A Jar 2

Sleep Between 3

Fate Fell Short 4

The Poem 5

Killing The Prom Queen 6

Death Of The Calendar 7

Broken Strings 8

Bleeding Hearts Shed No Tears 9

Whispers On The Wind 10

Echoes In The Abyss 11

Starlight Serenade 12

Moonlit Musings 13

Rhythms Of The Souls 14

Fractured Light 15

Beneath The Surface 16

Luminous Lines 17

Whispers In The Dark 18

Echoes Of Eternity 19

The Language Of Dreams 20

Bleeding Mascara 21

When Two Are One 22

Whispers Of The Cosmos 23

Soulscapes 24

Infinite Corridors 25

Ghost Of Eternity 26

The Memory Of Forgetting 27

Aurora Of The Unseen 28

A Bitter Broken Memory 29

When The Day Is Done 30

So Others May Live 31

Paper Castle...32

Anger Left Behind 33

Broken Again 34

Dead Weight 35

Watch Me Burn 36

Dancing With My Demons 37

Death Or Glory 38

The Beautiful Dark Of Life 39

To Kill Tomorrow 40

Forgiveness Is Murder 41

My Best Wishes 42

To Be Sleeping While Still Standing..............43

Say Goodbye 44

The Deepest Sleep 45

Beginning Of The End 46

The Beaten Path 47

Memento Vivere..48

Fade Away...49

World Falls Away 50

Simplest Mistake 51

Like Suicide..52

Rise Above This...53

Walk Away From The Sun...........................54

Left For Dead..55

Master Of Disaster 56

See You At The Bottom 57

Against The Wall 58

Let Me Heal 59

Nothing Left 60

Count Me Out 61

Emotionless...62

Dead And Done 63

Buried In The Sand....................................64

Drift Away 65

Pride Before The Fall 66

Calculating Infinity 67

Endless Endings 68

I wouldn't If You Didn't 69

Dead Throne 70

My Questions..71

Born To Lose...72

Forever Decay 73

Celestial Mechanics 74

The Sadness Will Never End 75

Dreamseeker 76

Lost In Silence 77

Pieces Of You In Me 78

Meeting Again For The First Time 79

Sounds Like The End Of The World 80

You Will Not Be Welcomed 81

The First Day Of My Second Life 82

When You Lose I Lose As Well 83

Truth In Separation 84

Light Years Away...85

In The Shadows 86

Burning Years 87

Divide And Conquer 88

Falling Down 89

Taste The Poison 90

Fight Against The World...91

March Of The Dead 92

Wake Up The Voiceless 93

A Silent Murder...94

Choose Your Fate 95

Angel In The Swamp 96

Ghost Of You And I...97

The Dream Is Over 98

Holding On To You 99

Time Goes On 100

Tonight We Fall 101

How Can We Go On 102

Can Anybody Hear Me 103

A Part Of Me 104

Give Up My Heart 105

To Be Alive Again 106

Praying For Rain 107

Tear Me To Pieces 108

Can't Save You 109

Sorry About Me 110

Unheard Voice 111

Falling Into Place 112

Perfection Through Silence 113

Without You Here 114

Stay With Me 115

Back To Oblivion 116

Further From The Few 117

The Great Divide 118

Something I Can Never Have 119

The Only Time 120

Beside You In Time 121

The Beginning Of The End 122

My Violent Heart 123

Another Version Of The Truth 124

Find My Way 125

Too Far Gone 126

My Paper Heart 127

Time Stands Still 128

Stab My Back 129

Move Along 130

Kiss Yourself Goodbye 131

Angel Cry 132

The Grim Goodbye 133

In Fate's Hands 134

False Pretense 135

Guardian Angel 136

You Better Pray 137

Lonely Road 138

Wake Me Up 139

Angel In Disguise 140

Don't Lose Hope 141

Fall From Grace 142

Forever Numb 143

Remember Me 144

Ignorance Is Bliss 145

Fighting Everything 146

The Awakening 147

Shooting Star 148

Unfinished Business 149

May Be Memories 150

On My Own 151

In Love And Death 152

All That I've Got 153

Yesterday's Feelings 154

Wake The Dead 155

Empty With You 156

Kissing You Goodbye 157

Broken Windows 158

The Divine Absence 159

The Quiet War 160

See You In Hell 161

Worst I've Ever Been 162

Dancing With A Brick Wall 163

House Of Sand 164

Depression Personified 165

Before I Leave 166

Dearly Departed.. 167

Late Goodbye 168

Everything Fades 169

Illusion And Dream 170

Dreaming Wide Awake 171

Given And Denied 172

Nothing Stays The Same 173

Shadow Play 174

The Labyrinth 175

Dancing On Broken Glass 176

The Sweet Escape 177

Moments Before The Storm 178

In A Perfect World... 179

Sounds Of Yesterday 180

Chasing Echoes 181

Weaver Of Dreams 182

Beyond The Horizon 183

Fairies Taste Like Machine Gun 184

Preface

In the uncharted territories of human experience, where the surreal and real converge, lies a realm of raw intensity and unflinching exploration. "Fairies Taste Like Machine Gun" is a poetic odyssey that delves into the complexities of our world, weaving together fragments of love, loss, and social commentary. This collection of poems is a cartography of the human condition, mapping the intricate landscapes of our inner lives.

Within these pages, tender moments and brutal truths coexist, inviting readers to confront the intricacies of existence. The poetry whispers secrets of resilience, survival, and the beauty hidden in darkness. It navigates the labyrinthine corridors of the human heart, exposing the contradictions and paradoxes that define us. With each verse, the boundaries between reality and fantasy blur, revealing the depths of our collective psyche.

Through a tapestry of words, the book reveals the fragility and strength of the human condition. It is an invitation to embark on a journey of self-discovery, to confront the shadows and embrace the light. The poems within these pages are a testament to the power of language to heal, to transform, and to transcend. Join this odyssey into the heart of our shared humanity, where the fantastical and real blur, and possibilities unfold.

As you delve into the world of "Fairies Taste Like Machine Gun", remember that the poems are not just words on a page, but a mirror held up to the human experience. May they reflect your deepest hopes, fears, and desires, and may they guide you toward a deeper understanding of yourself and the world around you.

Memento Mori

Fragile petals of existence
Dance in the breeze of time
Ephemeral whispers of what's past
Echoes of what's yet to unwind

In the mirror's silvered light
A stranger's face, a fading sight
Shadows creep, like silent thieves
Stealing moments, as the heart beats

Memories, like autumn leaves, rustle
Golden hues, of what's been lost
In the silence, a solitary bell
Tolls the passing, of all that's been told

Yet, in the depths of mortal fear
A strange solace, begins to appear
A reminder to cherish each breath
For in the end, only memories bequeath

In the stillness, a quiet voice
Whispers truths, of life's fragile choice
To hold dear, each fleeting moment
For in its beauty, our souls are made whole

Cosmos In A Jar

A universe contained,
Infinite within finite bounds,
Stardust swirls, a celestial storm,
Whispers of the cosmic sound.

Glittering fragments of the whole,
Dance in the darkness, a secret soul,
A miniature majesty, a tiny throne,
The cosmos shrunk, to fit the unknown.

In this glass prison, a world is free,
A swirling vortex, of possibility,
Gas and dust condense, a star is born,
A miniature miracle, in a tiny form.

The jar, a womb, a cosmic nest,
A place where wonder, is forever at rest,
The cosmos stirs, a gentle hum,
A reminder of the mystery to come.

In this small space, the universe expands,
A microcosm, of the infinite plans,
A cosmos in a jar, a wonder to behold,
A tiny window, to the secrets of the bold.

Sleep Between

In the realm of forgotten slumber,
Where dreams are lost, and shadows plunder,
A twilight world, of whispers grey,
Lies the sleeping soul, in disarray.

In this liminal space, where darkness reigns,
The mind wanders, through forgotten lanes,
Memories fade, like sand between the toes,
As the sleeper drifts, on a sea of woes.

The lost dreams whisper secrets in the night,
Forgotten tales, of a distant light,
Echoes of what could have been, or so it seems,
Haunting the sleeper, in a realm of dreams.

In this abyss of sleep, where shadows play,
The sleeper floats, in a world astray,
From the waking world, with all its pain,
To a realm of nothing, where dreams are vain.

Yet, in this void, a strange peace is found,
A solace from the world's loud sound,
A refuge from the light, that shines so bright,
A place to hide, from the darkness of night.

Fate Fell Short

Fragments of fate, like shattered glass,
Scattered dreams, and a future past,
A trajectory, once so clear and bright,
Now a labyrinth, of endless night.

In the cartography of destiny's design,
A wrong turn, a misstep, a fault line,
A crevice opened, and the path gave way,
To a chasm of uncertainty's gray.

Whispers of what could have been, a sigh,
Echoes of a future, that passed by,
A shadow of potential, lost in the haze,
A promise unkept, in the maze.

In the depths of what fell short, a silence reigns,
A stillness that echoes, with what remains,
A longing for a door, that closed too soon,
A regret for a chance, that slipped away, like moon.

Yet, in the shards of shattered fate,
A glimmer of freedom, begins to create,
A new trajectory, born of the broken,
A chance to rewrite, the unspoken.

The Poem

Ink whispers secrets, on the page's skin
A labyrinth of meaning, where words spin
A dance of symbols, a symphony of thought
Echoes of emotions, in the silence brought

The poem's pulse beats, like a heart in flight
A rhythm of revelation, in the dark of night
A tapestry of language, woven with care
A world of wonder, hidden in the words that share

In the poem's depths, a mirror's gaze
Reflects the soul's whispers, in a secret daze
A window to the self, where shadows roam
A journey through the psyche, to the heart's true home

The poem's essence, a mist that clings
To the edges of understanding, where truth sings
A haunting melody, that echoes through time
A fragment of the infinite, in the poem's rhyme

Killing The Prom Queen

A tiara lies shattered, on the floor's cold stage
A crown of beauty, lost in a bloody rage
The queen's sweet smile, now a haunting scream
A memory etched, in the killer's guilty dream

In the hall of mirrors, reflections stare
A thousand faces, of the one who dared
To take the life, of the one so fair
A secret kept, in the darkness shared

The prom's sweet melody, now a haunting refrain
Echoes of laughter, forever in vain
A night of joy, turned to endless pain
A memory that haunts, like a ghostly stain

In the silence, a whisper speaks
A truth revealed, in the killer's shriek
A secret kept, no more, no less
A prom queen's life, lost in a deadly caress

Death Of The Calendar

Time's skeletal hand, once held with care
Now withers, leaves scattered, beyond repair
Pages torn, days lost, months astray
A year's last breath, fades away

Ink bleeds, numbers blur, names forgotten
Memories linger, like shadows unspoken
The calendar's pulse, once beat with life
Now still, a relic, devoid of strife

Seasons merge, a never-ending haze
As chronos' chains, are broken, dazed
The death of time, a liberating sigh
Freedom from schedules, a timeless sky

In the void, a new rhythm's born
A cadence of moments, unsworn
Unshackled from dates, and hours' might
A dance with eternity, through the night

Broken Strings

Silken threads, once taut and fine
Now frayed, a discordant rhyme
Echoes of memories, lost in air
A symphony of sorrow, beyond repair

Vibrations cease, a haunting hush
A lonely silence, where music's rush
Fingers once danced, upon the fret
Now still, a melancholy regret

In the void, a whisper's sigh
A longing for harmony, to reunite
The shards of sound, a heart's deep pain
A yearning to weave, the fragments again

In the silence, a new refrain
A haunting beauty, a heart's deep strain
For in the broken, a truth is told
Of love, loss, and the beauty that grows old

Bleeding Hearts Shed No Tears

Silken threads of anguish weave a tapestry of pain
Crimson petals unfolding, a sorrowful bloom
Gossamer whispers of heartache echo through the void
A delicate, shattered vessel, containing the weight of grief

Fragile, lace-like fissures spread, a network of despair
A somber, twilight hue, settling upon the soul
In the depths of a wounded, cavernous space
A solitary, flickering ember, casts shadows of longing

Ethereal, misty veils, shroud the contours of the heart
A labyrinthine, winding path, navigates the darkness
In this desolate, barren landscape, a flower of sorrow blooms
Its beauty, a poignant, haunting melody, echoing through the silence

Whispers On The Wind

Echoes of the unseen, a gentle caress
A soft unfolding, of secrets and silence
The wind's dark fingers, tracing paths unseen
A hidden language, whispered to the heart's deep sheen

In the hollows of the air, a mysterious hush
A quiet summoning, of the soul's dark rush
The whispers weave, a tapestry of the unknown
A fragile, shimmering web, where truth is sown

In the whispering hours, when shadows softly fall
A lonely serenade, echoes through it all
A call to the hidden, a summons to the deep
A whispered promise, in the darkness, secrets keep

Echoes In The Abyss

In the void's dark embrace, a whispering begins
A labyrinthine murmur, where shadows spin
Echoes unfurl, like tendrils of a forgotten vine
A haunting reverberation, where silence is divine

In the abyss's hollow heart, a resonance resounds
A whispered litany, of forgotten sounds
The echoes swirl, a maelstrom of the past
A vortex of memories, forever meant to last

In the dark expanse, a lonely whisper calls
A haunting reminder, of forgotten falls
The echoes whisper, secrets to the night
A mysterious communion, in the abyss's dark light

Starlight Serenade

Celestial whispers, a gentle, ethereal hush
A twinkling tapestry, of light and shadow's rush
Stardust serenades, a heavenly, soft refrain
A cosmic waltz, where darkness is aflame

Glittering echoes, a chorus of light and sound
A symphony of stars, where silence is unbound
In the velvet expanse, a lonely melody calls
A siren's whisper, beckoning through the cosmic halls

Auroral harmonies, a shimmering, iridescent glow
A celestial ballet, where starlight whispers low
In the starry silence, a gentle, loving breeze
A serenade of light, where the heart finds its ease

Moonlit Musings

Lunar whispers, a silvered, gentle hue
A midnight reverie, where shadows dance anew
Moonbeams weave, a tapestry of dreams and thought
A nocturnal serenade, where the heart is caught

Gossamer threads, a fragile, shimmering net
A celestial snare, where musings are beset
In the moon's pale light, a lonely path unwinds
A winding journey, through the labyrinth of the mind

Ethereal echoes, a soft, whispery refrain
A lunar litany, where the soul's depths are gained
In the moonlit silence, a quiet, peaceful nest
A sanctuary of dreams, where the heart finds rest

Rhythms Of The Souls

Echoes of eternity, a symphony of the deep
A celestial cadence, where heartbeats softly creep
Invisible harmonies, a chorus of the unseen
A mystical resonance, where souls are serenely gleaned

Whispers of the cosmos, a rhythmic, pulsing tide
A universal heartbeat, where love and joy reside
In the secret chambers, of the soul's dark night
A luminous vibration, ignites the inner light

Ethereal oscillations, a dance of the divine
A sacred synchrony, where hearts and souls entwine
In the rhythms of the soul, a hidden truth is told
A mystical melody, that echoes through the ages old

Fractured Light

Shattered spectrums, a kaleidoscope of pain
A prism of broken dreams, refracting joy in vain
Splintered rays, a fractured, flickering glow
A light that's lost its way, in a world of shattered snow

Echoes of radiance, a haunting, ethereal sigh
A whispered promise, of a light that's yet to fly
In the shards of shadow, a glimmer still remains
A fractured beauty, that refuses to wane

Auroral fragments, a celestial, shimmering haze
A light that's broken, yet still finds its way
Through the cracks of darkness, a gentle, golden seep
A fractured light, that in its brokenness, still creeps

Beneath The Surface

Invisible tides, a hidden world below
A secret realm, where shadows softly grow
Unseen currents, a mysterious, dark design
A depth that's unexplored, where truth and silence entwine

Echoes of the unseen, a whispered, ethereal sigh
A haunting resonance, that only the heart can buy
In the stillness of the deep, a world of secrets sleep
A hidden universe, where mysteries softly creep

Beneath the surface, a labyrinth of the soul
A winding path, where shadows make us whole
In the darkness of the deep, a light begins to seep
A radiant awakening, that in the darkness, softly creep

Luminous Lines

Ethereal threads, a tapestry of light and space
A celestial cartography, mapping the unseen place
Glowing filaments, a network of radiance and might
A luminous labyrinth, guiding us through the dark of night

Invisible pathways, a shimmering, iridescent glow
A spectral topography, where shadows come to know
The contours of the soul, a terrain of light and shade
A luminous geography, where heart and spirit are made

Gossamer routes, a heavenly, shimmering haze
A luminous navigation, through life's winding ways
In the luminous lines, a hidden truth is told
A celestial blueprint, where heart and soul are made of gold

Whispers In The Dark

Shadowy murmurs, a mysterious, velvet hush
A secret language, spoken by the darkness' gentle rush
Echoes of the unknown, a whispered, ethereal sigh
A hidden world of whispers, where the heart's secrets reside

In the blackness of the night, a soft, whispery voice
A gentle, urgent murmur, that only the soul can choose
To listen to the whispers, that in the darkness play
A mystical, lunar litany, that guides us on our way

In the whispers of the dark, a hidden truth is shared
A mysterious, cosmic wisdom, that only the heart can spare
A language of the shadows, that speaks of secrets untold
A whispered, velvet promise, of mysteries yet to unfold

Echoes Of Eternity

Timeless whispers, a celestial, shimmering haze
A labyrinth of echoes, where eternity's secrets sway
Infinite corridors, a whispering gallery of the past
A mystical, echoing chamber, where moments forever last

Echoes of forever, a haunting, ethereal refrain
A whispered litany, of love and loss and joy and pain
In the halls of eternity, a soft, whispery voice is heard
A gentle, urgent murmur, that only the heart can absorb

Shadows of forever, a dark, shimmering tide
A mystical, echoing ocean, where moments are the guide
In the echoes of eternity, a hidden truth is told
A celestial, whispery promise, of forever to unfold

The Language Of Dreams

Silken threads of moonlight, weave a secret narrative
A mystic tongue that whispers truths, beyond the waking state
Ephemeral symbols dance, in the realm of the unknown
A hidden lexicon, where the heart's deepest mysteries are sown

In the dreamworld's labyrinthine corridors, a journey unfolds
A path of self-discovery, through the shadows of the soul
The language of dreams, a cryptic, shimmering mist
That veils and reveals, the secrets of the heart's deepest wish

Celestial cartography, mapping the inner terrain
A dreamlike topography, where the soul's mysteries remain
In this mystical realm, the heart's deepest truths reside
A secret language, that only the soul can decipher and hide.

Bleeding Mascara

Sorrow's dark rivulets, trickle down the face
A midnight waterfall, of tears and secret places
Black rivulets of heartache, like a summer storm's refrain
A melancholy mascara, that weeps, and weeps, in vain

In the mirror's silvered glass, a fragile, fractured gaze
A reflection of shattered dreams, in a pool of dark, mascara'd haze
Like a raven's call, the tears, a mournful, whispered sigh
A bleeding heart, that weeps, and weeps, and will not dry

In the mascara's dark, flowing streams, a story's told
Of love, loss, and longing, of a heart that's grown old
A fragile, flickering flame, that gutters, dimly, still
A bleeding mascara, that weeps, and weeps, and will not chill.

When Two Are One

Entwined essence, a symphony of souls
Two hearts, one rhythm, a celestial, swirling whole
Infinite threads, a tapestry of love's design
Interwoven destinies, a cosmic, beating rhyme

In the depths of each other's eyes, a mirrored universe resides
A reflection of the infinite, where love abides
Two paths, one journey, a harmonious, winding road
A sacred, symbiotic dance, where hearts are made to unfold

In the union of two, a new world is born
A fusion of essence, where love's alchemy is sworn
One love, one heart, one soul, a trinity of devotion
A bond that transcends, the boundaries of time and motion.

Whispers Of The Cosmos

Cosmic whispers hum
In the silence of the night
Mysteries untold

Stars whisper secrets
In the vast expanse above
Eternal wisdom

Galaxies whisper
A symphony of stardust
Echoes in the void

Soulscapes

Painted on our souls
Landscapes of love and sorrow
Memories linger

Mountains of triumph
Valleys of doubt and despair
Our souls bear the weight

Sunset hues of gold
Whispering winds through the trees
Soulscapes never fade

Infinite Corridors

Endless corridors
A never-ending maze goes
Lost in time and space

Walls stretch on and on
Twisting paths lead nowhere fast
Infinite confusion

No escape in sight
Eternal hallway of doors
Lost in corridors

Ghost Of Eternity

Fade into darkness
Ephemeral ghostly form
Whispers of forever

Silent specter haunts
Forever wandering lost
Echoes of the past

Shadowy figure
Lingering through endless time
A ghost of eternity

The Memory Of Forgetting

Fading like the mist
The memory of forgetting
Lost in time's embrace

Moments slip away
Like grains of sand in the wind
The past slowly fades

Echoes of a past
Whisper in the silent night
Lost to oblivion

Aurora Of The Unseen

Ethereal lights dance
Invisible to naked eye
Magic in the sky

Mysteries unfold
Auras unseen by all but
Those who seek with heart

Whispers in the night
Aurora of the unseen
Revealed to the soul

A Bitter Broken Memory

A broken memory
Bitter taste on my tongue lingers
Haunting me always

Each bitter moment
Embedded in my soul deep
Shadows never fade

Lost in bitter thoughts
Memories cut like sharp knives
Leaving scars unseen

When The Day Is Done

Sun dips below earth
Colors blend into the night
Day fades into dreams

Silent stars appear
Whispers of the day's goodbye
Peaceful night descends

Shadows lengthen, fade
Curtains close on the world's stage
Rest comes with the dusk

So Others May Live

Swift and selfless hearts
Risk it all to aid strangers
So others may live

Courageous heroes
Brave the storm to save a life
Their sacrifice shines

In darkness they shine
Angels on earth, hands of hope
For others they give

Paper Castle

Paper castle stands
fragile as a butterfly
dreams live within it

Whispers of laughter
echo through the paper halls
castle made of dreams

Fragile walls crumble
memories float like petals
paper castle falls

Anger Left Behind

Bitter words spoken
Anger lingers like a cloud
Long after it fades

Heart heavy with rage
Memories haunt like shadows
Anger consumes me

Forgiveness whispers
Anger slowly dissipates
Peace fills the void

Broken Again

Shattered heart once more
Pieces scattered on the floor
Trying to mend, tore

Fractured trust, so fragile
Promises now obsolete
Healing seems futile

Broken again, pain
Echoes through the emptiness
Hope seems a distant shore

Dead Weight

Heavy burden carried
Dead weight on tired shoulders
Strength fades away fast

Anchored to the past
Weight of regrets pulling down
Can't move forward now

Dead weight on my heart
Memories that won't let go
Dragging me under

Watch Me Burn

Embers glow brightly
watch me burn, consumed by flames
ashes left behind

Fiery passion burns
watch me ignite, fierce and wild
destructive beauty

Silent screams of pain
watch me suffer, engulfed by
the flames of my soul

Dancing With My Demons

In shadows we sway
to the rhythm of regret,
dancing with demons.

Twisting and turning,
their whispers fill the night air,
a haunting embrace.

Lost in their dark eyes,
we dance until the sunrise,
partners in pain.

Death Or Glory

The battle rages
Death or glory, life in hand
Courage will prevail

In the shadow's grasp
Glory whispers sweet nothings
Death's embrace so cold

A legacy fades
In the echoes of glory
Death's silent reward

The Beautiful Dark Of Life

In shadows we find
beauty, mystery, and grace
in the depth of night

Silent and serene
the darkness holds secrets deep
where light cannot reach

Embrace the unknown
find solace in the night's peace
life's beauty revealed

To Kill Tomorrow

Dread hangs in the air
Tomorrow's end swiftly nears
Life's thread snaps undone

Sharp blade glints with glee
Dark intent hides in shadows
Preparation done

Hushed whispers of fate
Tomorrow's sun won't rise again
Death's cold touch draws near

Forgiveness Is Murder

Forgiveness is hard
Like a murder of the self
Let go of the hurt

Blood stains on the hands
Of one who seeks redemption
Sacrifice for peace

Sharp words pierce the heart
But healing can still take place
Forgiveness is key

My Best Wishes

Sending wishes high
Filled with love and happiness
To light up your soul

Dreams unfolding bright
May your path be filled with light
Guiding you with love

Infinite blessings
Sprinkled upon your journey
Leading you to joy

To Be Sleeping While Still Standing

Heavy eyelids droop
Body swaying, barely awake
Sleeping while standing

Mind drifts off to dreams
Balance wavers, legs give way
Sleeping on my feet

Birds rest on branches
Slumbering in the moonlight
Standing still, at peace

Say Goodbye

Whispers in the wind,
A bittersweet farewell now,
Memories linger.

Parting is such sweet
Sorrow, a chapter closing,
New beginnings start.

Farewell, dear friend, gone
But not forgotten, always
In our hearts, goodbye.

The Deepest Sleep

Wrapped in darkness deep
Dreams like whispers in the night
Resting, peaceful, free

Silent slumber calls
Mind at rest, body in peace
Deepest sleep takes hold

Soft breath, gentle sigh
Sinking into oblivion
In the arms of sleep.

Beginning Of The End

Darkness on the brink
The edge of our final days
Beginning of the end

Whispers of farewell
Echo through the empty streets
Time slips away fast

Shadows lengthen now
Final chapter drawing near
Beginning of the end

The Beaten Path

Along the worn trail
Footsteps echo through the trees
Nature's ancient song

The path less traveled
Full of secrets yet untold
Adventure awaits

Beaten path weaves on
Through valleys and over streams
Guiding us back home

Memento Vivere

Life is a treasure
Each moment we must savor
Memento vivere

With each passing day
Embrace all the joys of life
Remember to live

In the present now
Seize the beauty that surrounds
Memento vivere

Fade Away

Colors slowly fade
Leaves wilt and fall to the ground
Summer ends, autumn

Memories will fade
Like footprints washed away by
The ocean's embrace

Time passes swiftly
Moments slip through fingertips
Life's colors fade out

World Falls Away

World falls away now
Only peace and silence left
In this quiet space

Cliffs meet the ocean
Water crashes against rocks
Nature's beauty clear

In the stillness here
I find peace in the chaos
World falls away now

Simplest Mistake

One step off the path,
the simplest mistake made,
lessons learned in time.

Words left unsaid, lost
in the void of silence, a
simplest mistake made.

A moment ignored,
the simplest mistake haunts me,
regrets fill my heart.

Like Suicide

Life's crushing weight
Swallows hope, consumes the light
Silent goodbye fades

Desperate whispers
Echo in the empty room
Fading breath, release

Darkness closes in
A final choice, ends the pain
Peace found in the void

Rise Above This

Rise above the noise
Focus on what truly counts
Find peace within you

Let go of the past
Embrace a brighter future
Soar high above doubt

You are stronger now
Face the challenges ahead
Rise above them all

Walk Away From The Sun

Walk away from sun's
blistering kiss, seek cool shade
and find peace within

Shadows grow longer
as the day begins to fade
whispers of night come

Escape the harsh light
and find solace in the dark
embrace the unknown

Left For Dead

In the dark forest
Left for dead without a trace
Will they find me here?

Abandoned and scared
Left for dead by those I trust
Loyalty shattered

Lost in the chaos
Left for dead, but I survive
Strength in solitude

Master Of Disaster

Master of chaos,
Creating destruction's path,
Leaving wreckage behind.

Disaster's puppeteer,
Pulling strings of mayhem and fear,
In his twisted game.

Controlled chaos reigns,
Master of disaster's art,
Leaving chaos in his wake.

See You At The Bottom

In the depths below
We'll meet again, you and I
Where shadows dance free

Underneath the waves
Our meeting place, silent and deep
Lost in the darkness

At the ocean's floor
We'll find each other once more
Until the next time

Against The Wall

Pressed against the wall
Silent screams trapped within me
No escape in sight

Desperation fades
As I lean against the wall
Seeking solace here

Whispers in the dark
Echo off the cold grey stone
Against the wall, lost

Let Me Heal

Silent tears that fall
Let me heal from all the pain
A new dawn will rise

Heartache fades away
Slowly finding peace within
Let me heal, embrace

Gentle whispers soothe
Healing light surrounds my soul
Let me heal, be free

Nothing Left

In empty silence
Nothing left to hold onto
Only memories

Fading into air
Nothing left but empty space
A void where you were

Whispers in the wind
Nothing left but echoes now
Gone without a trace

Count Me Out

I'll sit on the bench
Watching others take the lead
Count me out, I'm done

Not joining the fight
I'll stay on the sidelines, safe
Count me out, be free

No more words to speak
Silent observer I'll be
Count me out, at peace

Emotionless

Emotionless stone
Heart untouched by love or hate
A blank slate awaits

Eyes devoid of light
No joy, no pain, no sorrow
Soul remains empty

Hollow shell of man
Lost in the void of nothing
No feeling remains

Dead And Done

Life's light now extinguished
Echoes of memories fade
Dead and gone, a past

Silent shadows fall
Whispers of what once had been
Death is final now

Gone is yesterday
No more tears, no more laughter
Rest in peace, dear soul

Buried In The Sand

Sand grains whisper low
A secret hidden below
Memories buried

Footprints fade away
Lost in the grains of time passed
Silent echoes lie

Sunset paints the sky
Sealing secrets in the land
Buried dreams will rise

Drift Away

Drifting through the clouds
Lost in a sea of daydreams
Mind floats far away

Quietly adrift
Thoughts drift like autumn leaves fall
Serenity found

Drifting with the tide
Away from all worries now
Peace surrounds me

Pride Before The Fall

Pride stands tall and strong,
Blinded by its own glory,
Soon to crumble down.

Once mighty and proud,
Now humbled by its downfall,
Lessons learned too late.

High above it all,
Pride's arrogance left behind,
Crashes to the ground.

Calculating Infinity

Infinite numbers
Countless digits stretch onward
Mathematical wonder

Solve the equation
Endless patterns emerge forth
Infinity's grace

Mind cannot conceive
Endless, boundless, neverending
Infinite beauty

Endless Endings

The sun sets so slow
Each day fades into midnight
Endless endings bloom

Seasons come and go
Leaves fall, snowflakes gently drift
Time's cycle unspools

Infinite vistas
Endless horizons entwine
Life's end, a new start

I wouldn't If You Didn't

*I wouldn't if you
didn't, a dance of echoes
reflecting choices*

*In this tangled web
of reciprocity, we
find our true motives*

*Creating a bond
of shared understanding, we
move as one in trust*

Dead Throne

Crumbling stone and dust,
Once grand throne lies forgotten,
A kingdom long lost

Silent echoes of
The past linger in the depths
Of the empty hall

Once a seat of power,
Now a relic of the past,
The dead throne endures

My Questions

Seeking answers lost
In a sea of unknown truths
Questions fill my mind

Echoes in the night
Whispers of lingering doubt
Yearning for clarity

Fluttering doubts dance
Like butterflies in my mind
Seeking truth's sweet nectar

Born To Lose

Born to lose it all
Fate sealed from the very start
No way to escape

Life's cruel twist of fate
Forever destined to fail
Born to lose, we fall

Lost in the abyss
Born to lose, never to win
Our story is writ

Forever Decay

Eternal decay
Time erodes all things to dust
Beauty fades away

Nature's slow decline
Leaves wither and branches break
Earth's cycle of death

Memories decay
Fading into darkened past
Time forever steals

Celestial Mechanics

The moon's gentle pull
Guiding tides with precision
Celestial dance

Orbits in motion
Planets align in the sky
Perfect harmony

Gravity's force strong
Holding galaxies in place
Eternal balance

The Sadness Will Never End

Raindrops fall like tears
Silent sorrow in my heart
Endless dark clouds loom

Echoes of despair
Lost in the depths of my soul
Aching, never-ending

Loneliness consumes
Eternal longing remains
Sadness knows no end

Dreamseeker

In search of dreams bright
Seeker wanders through the night
Hoping for insight

Whispers of unknown
Guiding dreamseeker forward
Towards the sun's throne

Chasing shadows lost
Dreamseeker follows the light
In dreams, true paths crossed

Lost In Silence

Lost in silence now
Thoughts echo in empty space
Yearning for a voice

Solitude surrounds
Silence pressing down on me
Longing for connection

Silent whispers lost
In the vast expanse of time
Lost in silence, alone

Pieces Of You In Me

Fragments of your soul
Embedded in my being
Blend and intertwine

Your essence lingers
In every breath I exhale
A part of me, you

Two halves become one
In a symphony of love
Our hearts beat as one

Meeting Again For The First Time

Reunited souls
Meeting again for the first time
A spark ignites bright

Eyes locked in a gaze
Memories flood back so sweet
Time stands still for us

Laughter fills the air
Two hearts beating as one now
Destiny fulfilled

Sounds Like The End Of The World

Dark clouds fill the sky
Thunder roars like a war cry
End of the world nigh

Screams echo through streets
Bombs explode, chaos complete
Silent whispers fade

Rumbling earth, flames rise
Destruction meets our demise
End of days beckons

You Will Not Be Welcomed

Intruding on space
Uninvited, you linger
No welcome for you

Boundaries ignored
You overstep, unwelcome
Respect is lacking

Uninvited guest
Your presence not wanted here
Please leave, go away

The First Day Of My Second Life

Awakening new
Breathing in fresh beginnings
Second chance at life

Sunrise on my soul
Colors dance in the new light
Blossoming rebirth

Embracing the day
Like petals opening wide
Second life begins

When You Lose I Lose As Well

In sync we both fall
Your loss echoes in my heart
Our fates intertwined

Separated souls
Bound by shared defeat and pain
I mourn alongside

We are mirrors, you
Reflecting loss back to me
In unity we grieve

Truth In Separation

Truth in separation
Distance reveals what is real
Bond tested and proved

Heartache in absence
Exploring depths of longing
Truth found in silence

Separation's pain
Exposing raw honesty
Truth unraveled, seen

Light Years Away

Cosmic dreams unfold
Light years away, beyond reach
Infinite beauty

Stars twinkle and fade
As time bends and stretches far
Beyond our small world

Galaxies collide
Millions of light years away
Eternal dance of light

In The Shadows

In the darkened room
Shadows dance before my eyes
Whispers in the night

Silent figures lurk
Hiding in the shadowed depths
Watching, waiting, still

In the shadows cast
Mysteries unfold unseen
A world of secrets

Burning Years

Embers flicker bright
Old memories turn to ash
Time's flames never die

Years in flames below
Burning bridges behind us
New paths must be forged

Long, burning years gone
Leaving only smoke and dust
Future rises bright

Divide And Conquer

Divide and conquer
Strategies to break us apart
Unity will win

Sow seeds of discord
Watch as foes turn on themselves
Strength in division

One against the many
Powerful force splintered
Fragmented and weak

Falling Down

I stumble and trip
Gravity pulls me closer
Embrace the cold ground

Graceful as a swan
Butterflies in my stomach
Life's unexpected

Embrace the landing
Mistakes teach us to stand tall
Rise up, stronger now

Taste The Poison

Bitter on the tongue
Poisoned words leave a stain deep
Taste lingers for days

Sickly sweet deceit
A toxic flavor of lies
Poisoning the soul

The venom spreads wide
Infecting thoughts and feelings
Taste the poison's bite

Fight Against The World

Battles rage within
Against the world's cruelty
Courage lights the way

Fists clenched in anger
Defiant spirit fighting
For a better world

Warrior's heart strong
Facing trials with resolve
Victory awaits

March Of The Dead

The dead march in fall
Silent footsteps on the ground
Their whispers linger

Ghosts from the past rise
Haunting memories in time
Marching through the night

Eerie procession
Lost souls in eternal rest
March of the dead souls

Wake Up The Voiceless

Silent souls arise
Speak your truth, be heard at last
Break the chains of silence

Whispers in the dark
Awaken the voiceless ones
Let their stories shine

Time to break the spell
Raise your voice, be bold and brave
Silence no longer

A Silent Murder

Silent blade strikes true
Life extinguished in silence
Whispers in the night

No screaming, no sound
A heart stopped, a soul released
Quiet end of life

Blood spills without noise
A life taken in stillness
Silent killer strikes

Choose Your Fate

Fate's path lies ahead
Choices made with careful thought
Shape the life you lead

Doors open and close
Choosing which to enter now
Destiny unfolds

In the hands of time
Our fate lies within our grasp
Choose wisely, my friends

Angel In The Swamp

Lost in murky depths
An angel glows with grace
Hope blooms in the mire

Silver wings shimmer
Guiding light in darkness' hold
Peace amidst the vines

In the swamp's embrace
Heaven's messenger alights
Beauty in the muck

Ghost Of You And I

Whispers in the night
Your presence lingers with me
Haunted by your love

Shadows in the dark
Memories of us remain
Forever haunting

Ghost of you and I
Eternal love that won't die
A spectral embrace

The Dream Is Over

The dream is over
Reality sets in
Heart heavy with loss

Fading colors fade
Memories slip away fast
Leaving only gray

Echoes of laughter
Now replaced by silence
Dreams shattered like glass

Holding On To You

Holding on to you
Like a ship amidst the storm
Safe in your embrace

Your hand in mine, firm
An anchor in troubled times
Together we stand

Through life's twists and turns
We cling to each other tight
Forever bound, true

Time Goes On

Time marches forward
Days blend into memories
Life's endless cycle

Seasons come and go
Nature's rhythm never stops
Time flows endlessly

Clock ticks steadily
Moments passing one by one
Time waits for no one

Tonight We Fall

Under starlit sky
Tonight we fall into love
Hearts beating as one

Moonlight whispers soft
Embracing the darkness now
Together we soar

In each other's arms
Falling deeper into bliss
Tonight we are free

How Can We Go On

In the darkest night
We search for a guiding light
To show us the way

Through trials and tears
We find strength to persevere
And carry on brave

With hope in our hearts
We rise above the despair
And find joy once more

Can Anybody Hear Me

Echoes in the dark
Sound bouncing off empty walls
Can anybody hear?

Silent cries go out
Lost in a vast sea of noise
Will anyone know?

Whispers in the wind
Seeking someone to listen
Can anybody hear?

A Part Of Me

In my heart it lies
A part of me still hidden
Waiting to be found

Deep inside my soul
A piece of me remains quiet
Longing to be known

Through storm and through calm
This part of me will endure
An eternal flame

Give Up My Heart

I give up my heart
to find peace and let go of
pain that holds me tight

Letting go of love
to set my heart free and find
solace in goodbye

My heart surrendered
to the universe's will
and the path it leads

To Be Alive Again

Breath of new morning
Springtime blooms awaken joy
Life's sweet revival

Sunlight breaks the night
Echoes of laughter return
Hope born from the dawn

Heart beats with new life
A second chance to thrive now
Grateful for each breath

Praying For Rain

Raindrops fall softly,
Prayers whispered for sweet relief,
Desert blooms once more.

Dry earth parched and cracked,
Heavenly tears descend down,
Life springs forth anew.

Clouds gather above,
Hopeful hearts bow in fervent prayer,
Raindrops finally fall.

Tear Me To Pieces

Torn apart inside
Heart shattered into pieces
Saltwater rivers

Words cutting like knives
Pain sweeping over my soul
Torn to shreds by you

Breaking me apart
Fragments scattered in the wind
Tear me to pieces

Can't Save You

Frantic cries for help
But the darkness overwhelms
No one can save you

Desperate pleas ignored
Alone in a world of fear
No escape in sight

Trapped in your own mind
No one can hear your anguish
A silent scream fades

Sorry About Me

I messed up again
Please forgive my careless ways
I'm truly sorry

Words spoken in haste
Regret fills my heavy heart
I'm so sorry, love

I hurt you deeply
Please know I feel your pain too
Forgive me, my friend

Unheard Voice

Whispers in the wind
Silent cries go unnoticed
Echoes fade away

Words left unspoken
Lost in the vast sea of noise
Yearning to be heard

Unheard voices cry
Desperate for recognition
Silence swallows them

Falling Into Place

Pieces fall in line
Life's puzzle slowly reveals
Destiny's design

Like a leaf adrift
Drifting towards its still pond
Falling into place

Stars align above
Guiding us towards our fate
Everything fits right

Perfection Through Silence

Silence speaks volumes
Perfection found in stillness
Words are unnecessary

In quiet moments
Perfection can be achieved
Through peaceful silence

Embrace the silence
Find perfection in the hush
Let tranquility reign

Without You Here

In the empty room
your absence is a weight
that I cannot bear

Silence echoes loud
without your laughter to fill
the space between us

Alone in my thoughts
wishing you were here with me
to chase away fears

Stay With Me

Stay with me always
In the darkness of the night
Let our love ignite

Hold my hand so tight
Together we'll brave the storm
In each other's light

Stay with me, my love
In each moment, by my side
Our hearts beat as one

Back To Oblivion

Back to oblivion
Lost in the depths of the mind
Fading memories

Silent whispers fade
Echoes of the past grow dim
Lost in shadows now

Into the void, gone
Forgotten in passing time
Back to oblivion

Further From The Few

Further from the few
Lost in a vast expanse
Unknown paths I choose

Silent whispers call
Echoes of distant lands
Beyond my reach now

Seeking solace far
In the shadows of the past
A distant light glows

The Great Divide

Among rolling hills
A chasm splits the landscape
Separates our worlds

On one side we stand
Yearning to bridge the divide
But fear holds us back

Through the great divide
We find unity in love
A bridge forever

Something I Can Never Have

Longing for your touch
But distance keeps us apart
My heart forever breaks

Dreams of you linger
In my thoughts, you are with me
Yet reality fades

Eternal yearning
For a love that cannot be
Unattainable

The Only Time

In the still of night
Time stands still, only for us
Love's eternal light

Time stops in your arms
Lost in your eyes, I'm at peace
Only you and me

Moments shared with you
The only time that matters
Forever in love

Beside You In Time

In harmony's grasp,
Beside you in time we stand,
Heartbeats synchronized.

Whispers of the past,
Echoes of our shared moments,
Forever entwined.

Through trials and triumphs,
Together we face the world,
Bound by fate and love.

The Beginning Of The End

Storm clouds gather near
Whispers of the end draw near
A new chapter starts

Seeds of decay sow
The end creeping ever close
Change is on the wind

Sunsets fade to black
The end of light draws near now
A new dawn beckons

My Violent Heart

Eager to break free
Beats like thunder in my chest
Violence within me

Raging tempest roars
Colliding against my ribs
Screams of agony

A beast lurks within
Clawing to tear me apart
My violent heart cries

Another Version Of The Truth

An alternate view
Truth bends and shifts like shadows
Light reveals the lie

In a mirror world
Facts become skewed and twisted
A different truth forms

Perspectives collide
Two sides of the same story
Where does reality lie?

Find My Way

Lost in the darkness
I search for a guiding light
To find my way home

A winding path waits
I follow footsteps unseen
Towards a new dawn

Through shadows I roam
But I trust the stars above
To guide me safely

Too Far Gone

Caught in the darkness
Lost in pity and despair
Too far gone to save

Bitter words spoken
Bridges burned, hearts left broken
Regrets fill the void

Memories of love
Fade away in the distance
Too far gone to find

My Paper Heart

Fragile paper heart
Torn by harsh words and actions
Yet still beats with love

Ink stains and creases
Show my heart's journey through life
Filled with highs and lows

Handle with such care
For my paper heart is small
But holds much love inside

Time Stands Still

In the quiet hush
Moments suspended in air
Time stands still, unmoved

Sunset's golden glow
Freezes the world in its light
Eternal moment

Clock's hands frozen, still
Silent ticking in the air
Holding time at bay

Stab My Back

Knife pierces my skin
Betrayal cuts deep within
Stabbed in the back, friend

Trust shattered in two
Words that wound, pain still stings
Friend turned enemy

Sharp blade in the night
Back turned, a silent attack
Betrayed by my own

Move Along

Moving along now
Leaving the past behind me
New adventures wait

Footprints in the sand
Each step leads to the unknown
Journey never ends

Letting go of fear
Embracing the path ahead
Move along with grace

Kiss Yourself Goodbye

Kiss yourself goodbye
Letting go of past regrets
Embrace the unknown

Whispers of farewell
Echo in the quiet room
Goodbye to old self

Embrace the new day
Kiss goodbye to the old ways
Welcome change with love

Angel Cry

Cries from angels' hearts
Tear-streaked faces in the sky
Their sorrow profound

Heaven's tears fall
Angels weep for lost souls
Silent prayers ascend

Thunderous sobs ring
Angels mourn earthly sorrows
Embracing the hurt

The Grim Goodbye

Whispers of farewell
Echo through the somber air
Parting ways with grief

Silent tears cascade
As we bid adieu to love
Heart heavy with loss

A somber farewell
Leaves a void in my being
Grim goodbye takes hold

In Fate's Hands

In fate's firm embrace
We surrender our control
Trust in the unknown

Destiny unfolds
Threads of life interwoven
Only time will tell

Paths intertwining
A dance of chance and choice made
Fate's design unseen

False Pretense

Fake smiles conceal lies
Masks worn to deceive others
Truth hidden within

False fronts crumbling
Hiding the cracks with façade
Deception revealed

Pretending to care
But motives are self-serving
True colors shine through

Guardian Angel

Whispers in the wind
Guiding me through darkest times
Angel by my side

Invisible friend
Watching over me always
Guardian angel

Soft wings wrap around
Protecting, comforting me
My angel unseen

You Better Pray

Pray for strength and hope
In the darkest hours of life
Faith will guide you through

Find solace in prayer
A refuge in troubled times
Hope shining brightly

In moments of fear
Let your faith be your anchor
Pray for peace within

Lonely Road

Lonely road stretches
Morning mist clings to the trees
Silence fills the air

Footsteps echo soft
Concrete whispers secrets kept
Loneliness surrounds

Moonlight guides the way
Stars twinkle in empty sky
Lonely road ahead

Wake Me Up

Eyes flutter open
Morning light floods into room
Wake me from slumber

Birds sing outside my window
Their melody beckons me
Rise from bed, embrace

Alarm clock buzzing
Time to greet the new day
Wake me up gently

Angel In Disguise

An angel in plain
clothes walks among us, unseen
bringing light and love

Eyes filled with kindness
A smile that warms the coldest
hearts, pure and divine

Humble servant, hidden
grace shines from within, a light
guiding us to peace

Don't Lose Hope

In the darkest night
a flicker of hope remains
guiding us to light

Clouds hide the sunlight
but remember, it still shines
hope will see us through

Beneath stormy skies
hope is a beacon of light
guiding us to peace

Fall From Grace

Fallen from high grace
A dark shadow now looms near
Lost in sorrow's embrace

Once held in esteem
Now cast out, left to wither
A soul adrift, lost

A fleeting moment
A fall from grace, a deep plunge
Lost in shame's cruel grip

Forever Numb

Emotionless heart
Forever numb, feeling cold
No tears left to cry

Pain fades into void
Numbness settles deep within
Lost in empty world

Forever numb mind
Silent screams, never breaking
Aching in stillness

Remember Me

In memories past
Fading like a distant dream
Will you remember?

Whispers in the wind
Echoes of a love once shared
Remember me now

Photos worn and old
Moments frozen in time's grasp
Forever cherished

Ignorance Is Bliss

Ignorance is bliss
Blissful unawareness brings
Peace in oblivion

Minds clouded by doubt
Shielded from harsh truths of life
Content in darkness

Bliss in ignorance
Unaware of the chaos
Happiness achieved

Fighting Everything

Steel clashes with bone
A battle fought within self
Conquer resistance

Anger sparks the flame
Rage against the dying light
Warrior within

Every obstacle
A challenge to be conquered
Victory rings out

The Awakening

Awakening light
Heralds the dawn of a new day
Nature stirs to life

Birds sing, flowers bloom
A symphony of rebirth
Hope blossoms anew

Eyes flutter open
To the beauty of morning
Awakening soul

Shooting Star

Streak of light above
Shooting star, grant me a wish
Fleeting beauty fades

Midnight sky aglow
Whispers of dreams come alive
Graceful star falls low

Wish upon a star
Magic in the night sky above
Shooting star's soft glow

Unfinished Business

Unfinished puzzles
Pieces scattered, thoughts untamed
What was left undone

Promises broken
Echoes of words left unsaid
Regrets linger on

Incompletion looms
Like a shadow, always near
Unfinished endings

May Be Memories

Sweet memories fade
Like the setting sun's colors
Glowing in my mind

Echoes of laughter
Drift through the quiet stillness
Of nostalgia's grasp

Whispers of the past
Haunt my thoughts like shadows cast
By a fading light

On My Own

Alone in silence
Thoughts drift through my empty mind
Lost in solitude

Walking down the street
Feeling lonely but at peace
Embracing solace

In my own world now
Finding peace in solitude
Content in my thoughts

In Love And Death

In love's sweet embrace
Even death cannot divide
Our souls intertwined

In death's cold embrace
Love's memory still lingers
Eternal flame burns

Love blooms in the heart
Death's shadow cannot conquer
Together forever

All That I've Got

Mountains rise above
All that I have is my love
Boundless as the sky

Laughter fills my days
Joy, the only thing that stays
All that I've got, praise

Memories so sweet
In my heart, they will repeat
All that I've got, complete

Yesterday's Feelings

Clouds blocked out the sun
Shadows of doubt lingered on
Lost in yesterday

Memories haunt me
Whispers of what could have been
Longing for closure

Heart heavy with grief
Yearning for a brighter day
Yesterday's feelings

Wake The Dead

Awaken the dead,
Beneath the pale moonlight's glow,
Their spirits now rise.

Whispers on the wind,
Echoes of the past arise,
Brought back from the grave.

Silent graves disturbed,
Ancient souls now walk again,
In the realm of night.

Empty With You

Emptiness within
A void that you used to fill
Now I am alone

Memories linger
Of laughter and love we shared
Now just emptiness

Silence like a ghost
Echoes of your absence here
My heart feels empty

Kissing You Goodbye

Tender lips touching
Saying our fond farewell kiss
Heartache lingers on

Whispers of parting
Wishing for one last embrace
Memories linger

Softly we embrace
Sweet sorrow in our farewell
Kissing you goodbye

Broken Windows

Shattered glass sparkles
Sunlight filtering through cracks
Beauty in chaos

Splintered shards of glass
Whispers of past memories
Echo through empty pane

Broken windows weep
Silent tears of shattered dreams
Lost in the debris

The Divine Absence

In the empty sky,
no gods or angels appear,
just silence reigns here.

In the void, we seek
answers from the universe,
but find only dark.

The divine absence
leaves us questioning our faith,
lost in uncertainty.

The Quiet War

Silent battle cries
Whispers of conflict unheard
Peace lost in stillness

Words unsaid linger
In the quiet war within
Hearts heavy with strife

Deafening silence
A war waged in hushed shadows
Lost souls cry in peace

See You In Hell

Fiery depths await
See you in hell, my old friend
Eternal torment

Demon's laughter rings
Echoing through fiery pit
See you in hell's grasp

Forsaken, we part
See you in hell, bitter end
Lost souls drift apart

Worst I've Ever Been

Heavy heart burdened
By the weight of my mistakes
Worst I've ever been

Shadows loom, darkness
Swallows me whole, drowning deep
In the depths of shame

Lost in a dark void
Clawing desperately for light
Worst I've ever been

Dancing With A Brick Wall

Dancing with a wall
Brick cold against warm fingers
Creating new groove

Smashing into stone
Rhythm echoes off the walls
Finding grace in strength

Brick wall stands unmoved
While I twirl and leap around
Dancing in my mind

House Of Sand

House of sand stands tall
Shifting with each gust of wind
Fragile and fleeting

Windows of glass blur
The line between inside, out
Lost in swirling grains

Foundation erodes
Time and nature take their toll
Whispers in the wind

Depression Personified

In shadows he dwells
A heavy weight on his chest
Silent screams go unheard

Whispers in his ears
Telling him he's worthless, lost
Darkness engulfs him

A ghost in his eyes
Haunted by his own sorrow
Depression's cruel grip

Before I Leave

Before I depart,
Memories flood my mind, tears
Fall like autumn leaves

Whispers of goodbye
Haunt me in the still night air
Echoes of lost love

Leaving behind me
A piece of my heart still lingers
In the quiet dawn

Dearly Departed

Whispers in the wind
Memories of those we loved
Echo through the trees

Gone but not forgotten
Their spirit lives on within
In hearts, forever

Tears fall like raindrops
As we bid our final farewell
To those who have gone

Late Goodbye

Saying goodbye late
Tears fall as we part our ways
Memories linger

Clock ticks as we pause
Regret fills the empty space
Words left unspoken

The sun sets too soon
Farewell comes with a heavy heart
Echoes of our past

Everything Fades

Colors fade to grey
Memories drift away too
Time takes all from us

Leaves fall from the trees
Seasons change and pass us by
Nothing stays the same

Like a fleeting dream
Life's beauty fades with time's touch
Cherish each moment

Illusion And Dream

Floating in a dream
Illusions dance before me
Reality fades

Mirage of desire
Haunting shadows in moonlight
Whispers of the heart

Lost in a daydream
Chasing elusive visions
Fleeting as the wind

Dreaming Wide Awake

Dreams dance before eyes
While the world sleeps soundly on
Imagination soars

Reality blurs
As visions take control
Mind's tapestry weaves

Awake in a dream
Bound by no earthly limit
Free to explore all

Given And Denied

Whispered promises
Torn apart by cruel fate's hand
Love's sweet joy turned sour

Heart filled with hope's light
Crushed by the weight of despair
Dreams fade into dusk

Denied the warmth of
Love's embrace, left cold and lost
Yearning for solace

Nothing Stays The Same

Life's ever-changing
Nothing stays the same for long
Embrace the unknown

Seasons come and go
Leaves fall, trees blossom anew
Nature's constant dance

Time moves endlessly
But we must learn to let go
And find peace within

Shadow Play

Shadows dance on wall
Figures trapped in flickering light
A story untold

Silhouettes intertwine
Creating shapes of beauty
In darkness they shine

Hands become puppets
Twisting and turning with grace
A show in shadow

The Labyrinth

A maze of stone walls
Twisting paths lead lost souls through
Searching for the light

Confusion reigns here
Eyes wide in the twisting dark
Lost in the maze's heart

Threads of fate untwine
Guide me through the labyrinth
Lead me to the end

Dancing On Broken Glass

Twirling on shards of
glass, pain forgotten in the
rhythm of the dance

Blood stains the floor, but
feet keep moving in tune with
the broken melody

Each step a gamble
on shattered glass, but still we
dance with reckless joy

The Sweet Escape

Drifting on a cloud
Away from chaos and noise
Peaceful solitude

Whispers of the wind
Carrying me far from here
To a hidden place

In the quiet spaces
I find solace and release
A sweet escape, free

Moments Before The Storm

Dark clouds start to form
Nature's fury is coming
Silence fills the air

Wind whispers softly
Trees sway in anticipation
Birds seek shelter soon

Lightning flashes bright
Thunder rolls in the distance
Storm is on its way

In A Perfect World

In a perfect world,
Unity and love would reign
Bringing peace to all

Nature in balance
Harmony is restored
Beauty surrounds us

In a perfect world
Hearts and minds are open wide
Hope and joy abound

Sounds Of Yesterday

Whispers in the wind
Echoes of laughter linger
Memories replay

Birds sing in the trees
Children's laughter fills the air
Sounds of joy remain

Chimes in the distance
Echoes of a distant past
Haunting melodies

Chasing Echoes

Chasing echoes long,
Whispers in the empty halls,
Fleeting memories.

Footsteps follow close,
But the sound always escapes,
A never-ending chase.

Echoes bounce and fade,
Lost in the vast expanse,
A haunting refrain.

Weaver Of Dreams

Through the night she weaves
threads of dreams with gentle hands
painting skies with stars

In her loom of light
weaver spins tales of wonder
whispers of the night

Dreams take flight on wings
crafted by the master weaver
guiding us to sleep

Beyond The Horizon

The sun sets beyond
the horizon, painting skies
in colors of flame.

Mysterious world
awaits just beyond the reach
of our wandering gaze.

Dreams drift like clouds past
the horizon, where the mind
wanders freely on.

Fairies Taste Like Machine Gun

Fairies on the wing
Taste of smoke and metal clang
Machine guns in flight

Tiny sprites aflutter
Metallic tang upon tongues
Fairy bullets sing

Sweetness stained with steel
Fairies dart and bullets fly
Machine gun magic